W9-DGV-400

Ready for
Division

Rebecca Wingard-Nelson

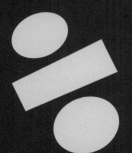

Enslow Elementary

an imprint of

Enslow Publishers, Inc.

E

40 Industrial Road
Box 398
Berkeley Heights, NJ 07922
USA

http://www.enslow.com

Enslow Elementary, an imprint of Enslow Publishers, Inc.

Enslow Elementary® is a registered trademark of Enslow Publishers, Inc.

Original edition published as *Division Made Easy* in 2005.

Library of Congress Cataloging-in-Publication Data

Wingard-Nelson, Rebecca.
 [Division made easy]
 Ready for division / Rebecca Wingard-Nelson; illustrations, Tom LaBaff.
   pages cm.— (Ready for math)
 Previously published as: Subtraction made easy. ©2005.
 Summary: "Learn the properties of division with such topics as inverse operations, key words, interpreting remainders, and dividing great numbers"— Provided by publisher.
 Includes bibliographical references and index.
 ISBN 978-0-7660-4249-0
 1. Division—Juvenile literature. I. LaBaff, Tom, illustrator. II. Title.
 QA115.W755 2014
 513.2'12—dc23
                                                           2012038511

Future editions:
Paperback ISBN: 978-1-4644-0441-2
Single-User PDF ISBN: 978-1-4646-1240-4

EPUB ISBN: 978-1-4645-1240-7
Multi-User PDF ISBN: 978-0-7660-5872-9

Printed in the United States of America

102013 Lake Book Manufacturing, Inc., Melrose Park, IL

10 9 8 7 6 5 4 3 2 1   6559

To Our Readers: We have done our best to make sure all Internet addresses in this book were active and appropriate when we went to press. However, the author and the publisher have no control over and assume no liability for the material available on those Internet sites or on other Web sites they may link to. Any comments or suggestions can be sent by e-mail to comments@enslow.com or to the address on the back cover.

Illustration Credits: Tom LaBaff
Cover Illustration: Tom LaBaff

Contents

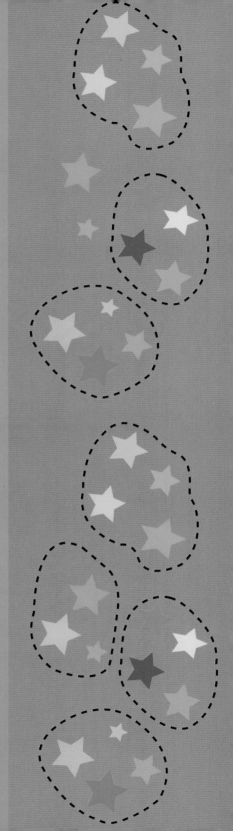

Introduction

Math is all around, and an important part of your life. You use math when you are playing games, cooking food, spending money, telling time, reading music, and doing any other activity that uses numbers. Even finding a television station uses math!

Division Is Everywhere

You use division in everyday life. When you split a bag of candy or a box of cookies with a friend, you are dividing. When you decide how many rows of seats your class will need during an assembly, you are dividing. Any time you have a group of things and need to separate them into smaller equal groups, you are dividing.

Using This Book

This book can be used to learn or review division at your own speed. It can be used on your own or with a friend, tutor, or parent. Get ready to discover math . . . made easy!

What Is Division?

Division is a way to break something into equal parts.

You have 20 king cobras. A basket holds 5 cobras. How many baskets do you need to hold all of your king cobras?

There are two ways to find the answer.

1 You can find the number of baskets by subtracting 5 cobras at a time from the total.

$$20 - 5 = 15 \qquad 1 \text{ basket}$$
$$15 - 5 = 10 \qquad 2 \text{ baskets}$$
$$10 - 5 = 5 \qquad 3 \text{ baskets}$$
$$5 - 5 = 0 \qquad 4 \text{ baskets}$$

You need 4 baskets to hold all 20 king cobras.

2 You can divide. Division is just another way to subtract over and over again.

20 divided by 5 is 4.

Division is repeated subtraction.

20 king cobras, divided into baskets of 5 snakes each, will fill 4 baskets.

Why Divide?

Suppose you know a total number of items. You also know the number of groups you want to equally put them into. You can divide to find how many items will be in each group.

Three friends bought a pizza. The pizza had six slices. If three friends shared the pizza equally, how many slices did each friend eat?

Six slices of pizza, divided equally among three friends, gave each friend two slices.

Six divided by three is two.

$$6 \div 3 = 2$$

Suppose you know the total number of items, and how many are in each group. You can divide to find the number of groups.

You have ten bees. You want to divide them into groups of two bees. How many groups can you make?

You can make 5 groups of 2 bees.

Ten divided by two is five.

$$10 \div 2 = 5$$

Division Terms

Suppose you have 18 pencils. You want to divide them into groups of 6. How many groups will you have?

The number 18 is the dividend.
It is the number being divided.

The number 6 is the divisor.
It is the number you divide by.

The answer to a division problem is called the quotient.
If you make groups of 6 pencils, you will have 3 groups.

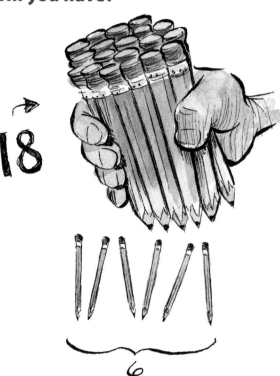

$$18 \div 6 = 3$$

When you read a division problem out loud, you say,

$$18 \div 6 = 3$$

Eighteen divided by three equals six.

Division can be shown using three different symbols.

The symbol $\div$ is called the division symbol.

$$18 \div 6 = 3 \quad \text{dividend} \div \text{divisor} = \text{quotient}$$

The fraction bar, —, also shows division.

$$\frac{18}{6} = 3 \qquad\qquad \frac{\text{dividend}}{\text{divisor}} = \text{quotient}$$

Division is also shown using $\overline{)}$, the long division symbol.

$$6\overline{)18}^{\,3} \qquad\qquad \text{divisor}\,\overline{)\,\text{dividend}}^{\,\text{quotient}}$$

All three ways of writing division problems are read the same way.

Eighteen divided by three equals six.

Division and Multiplication

Division and multiplication are inverse operations. They undo each other's work.

Multiplication says six times three is eighteen.

$$6 \times 3 = 18$$

Division says eighteen divided by three is six.

$$18 \div 3 = 6$$

Multiplication puts equal groups together. Division breaks a whole into equal groups.

operation—An action that works to change a number.
inverse operations—Operations that undo each other.

Multiplication is repeated addition. Division is repeated subtraction.

Three rows of four chairs
make a total of twelve chairs.

$$3 \times 4 = 12$$

Twelve chairs divided into
rows of four chairs each
will fill three rows.

$$12 \div 4 = 3$$

That's a lot of chairs.

Division Facts

You can learn division facts by using the multiplication facts.
Let's review the terms for multiplication.

$$\text{factor} \times \text{factor} = \text{product}$$
$$3 \quad \times \quad 7 \quad = \quad 21$$

Let's look at the same fact, written using division.

$$\text{product} \div \text{factor} = \text{factor}$$
$$\text{(dividend)} \div \text{(divisor)} = \text{(quotient)}$$
$$21 \quad \div \quad 7 \quad = \quad 3$$

When you know the multiplication fact $3 \times 7 = 21$,
then you also know the division fact $21 \div 7 = 3$.

Remember: In multiplication, you can change the order of the factors, and the answer is the same.

For each multiplication fact you know, you really know four facts.

When you know $3 \times 7 = 21,$

you also know $7 \times 3 = 21,$

$21 \div 3 = 7,$

and $21 \div 7 = 3.$

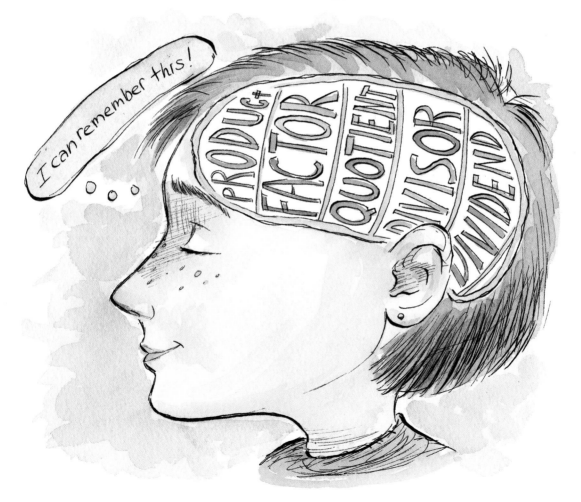

Zero and One

No number can be divided by zero. Look at the division problem below.

$$6 \div 0 = \underline{\quad 6 \quad}$$

The problem is asking, How many groups of zero items will make six items? You could have as many groups of zero as you want and still never have a total of six.

On the other hand, zero can be divided by any number. The answer will always be zero. If you have nothing (zero) and divide it into any number of equal groups, there will be nothing (zero) in each group.

$$0 \div 2 = 0$$

$$0 \div 27 = 0$$

$$0 \div 312 = 0$$

Any number divided by one stays the same number.

If you have eight baseballs and divide them into one equal group, the group will have eight baseballs in it.

$$8 \div 1 = 8$$

When any number is divided by itself, the answer is one.

If you have nine beads and divide them into groups of nine, how many groups will you have? You will have one group.

$$9 \div 9 = 1$$

Long Division

Sometimes you need to divide numbers that are not basic facts. You can use long divison.

$$42 \div 3 \text{ is written as } 3\overline{)42}.$$

Divide one place value at a time, beginning on the left.

divisor $\searrow 3\overline{)42}$ Divide 3 into the first digit of the dividend (42).
dividend

How many groups of 3 can you make from 4? Find the 3s multiplication fact with an answer closest to 4, but not greater than 4.

$$3 \times 1 = 3 \qquad\qquad 3 \times 2 = 6$$

There is one group of 3 in 4. Two groups of 3 is greater than 4.

$\times\! 1$
$3\overline{)42}$
$=\! 3$ Write a 1 in the answer above the 4.

Multiply the number you just wrote (1) by the divisor (3).

$1 \times 3 = 3$. Write the 3 below the 4.

18

```
  1
3)42
 − 3
 ───
   1
```

Subtract. 4 − 3 = 1. In long division, the difference (1) must be less than the divisor (3). 1 is less than 3.

```
  1
3)42
 − 3↓
 ───
  12
```

Bring down the next number (2). Now you have the number 12. Divide 3 into 12. (Think: How many groups of 3 can I make from 12?)

The number 12 will make exactly 4 groups of 3 (4 × 3 = 12).

```
   ×
   14
 3)42
=( − 3
   ───
    12
  − 12
  ────
     0
```

Write a 4 above the 2.
Multiply. 4 × 3 = 12.
Write the product (12) below the 12.
Subtract. 12 − 12 = 0.
There are no more numbers to bring down.
You are finished!

$$42 \div 3 = 14$$

Dividing Greater Numbers

You can divide any number by a one-digit number using long division.

$294 \div 6$ is written as $6\overline{)294}$.

divisor $\searrow$ $6\overline{)294}$
dividend

In the dividend, the first number on the left is 2.
The number 2 is smaller than 6, so you cannot make any groups of 6 from 2.

$6\overline{)294}$

The next number is 9. Since you did not use the 2, the number you are looking at is 29. The number 29 will make 4 groups of 6 ($4 \times 6 = 24$), but not 5 ($5 \times 6 = 30$).

$$
\begin{array}{r}
4 \\
6\overline{)294} \\
-24 \\
\hline
5
\end{array}
$$

Write a 4 above the 9.
Multiply. $4 \times 6 = 24$.
Write 24 below the 29.
Subtract. $29 - 24 = 5$.

$$\begin{array}{r} 4 \\ 6)\overline{294} \\ -\ 24 \\ \hline 54 \end{array}$$

Bring down the next number, 4. Now you have 54. The number 54 will make exactly 9 groups of 6 ($9 \times 6 = 54$).

$$\begin{array}{r} 49 \\ 6)\overline{294} \\ -\ 24 \\ \hline 54 \\ -\ 54 \\ \hline 0 \end{array}$$

Write a 9 above the 4.

Multiply. $9 \times 6 = 54$.

Write the product (54) below the 54.

Subtract. $54 - 54 = 0$.

There are no more numbers to bring down.

You are finished!

$$294 \div 6 = 49$$

Wow! That's easy.

What Are Remainders?

You have nine blueberry muffins. You want to put the muffins in boxes. If you put four muffins in each box, how many boxes do you need?

You will need 2 boxes with 4 muffins in each, but there would be one muffin left over.

When there is a number left over in division, it is called a remainder.

Use long division to find division answers with remainders.

$$30 \div 9 \text{ is written as } 9\overline{)30}.$$

$9\overline{)30}$ Look at the first number. Can you make a group of 9 from 3? No. Look at the next number. The number, 30, will make 3 groups of 9 ($3 \times 9 = 27$), but not 4($4 \times 9 = 36$).

$$\begin{array}{r} 3 \\ 9\overline{)30} \\ -27 \\ \hline 3 \end{array}$$

Write 3 above the 0.
Multiply. $3 \times 9 = 27$.
Write 27 below the 30.
Subtract. $30 - 27 = 3$.
There are no more places to divide, so the remainder is 3.

$$\begin{array}{r} 3 \text{ R}3 \\ 9\overline{)30} \\ -27 \\ \hline 3 \end{array}$$

Write the remainder in the answer using an R to show it is a remainder.

$$30 \div 9 = 3 \text{ R}3$$

23

The Largest Remainder

The largest remainder that a division problem can have is one number less than the divisor.

remainder–The number left over in a division problem.

For example, if you are dividing by 4, the largest remainder you can have is 3. Let's look at two problems and see why.

How many groups of 4 stars can you make from 15 stars?

You can make 3 groups of 4 with 3 stars left over.

$$15 \div 4 = 3 \text{ R}3$$

If you had one more star in the original group, there would be 16 stars.

How many groups of 4 stars can you make from 16 stars?

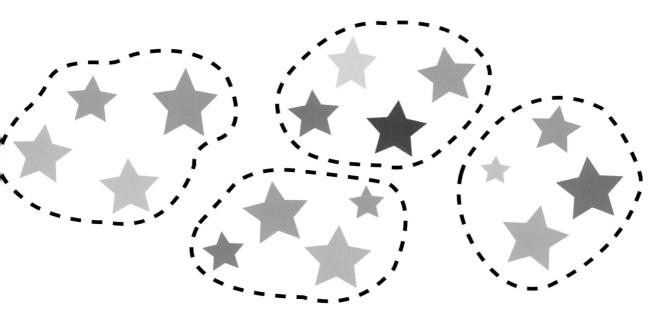

You can make exactly 4 groups of 4 stars.

$$16 \div 4 = 4$$

When you divide by 4, the largest remainder you can have is 3.

If you have more than 3, you can make another group.

Dividing by Greater Numbers

Use long division to divide by larger numbers.

$$2{,}154 \div 16 \text{ is written as } 16\overline{)2154}.$$

$16\overline{)2154}$

Look at the first number. Can you make a group of 16 from 2? No. Look at the next number. You can make 1 group of 16 ($1 \times 16 = 16$) from 21, but not 2 ($2 \times 16 = 32$).

$$\begin{array}{r} 1 \\ 16\overline{)2154} \\ -\,16 \\ \hline 5 \end{array}$$

Write a 1 above the 1.
Multiply. $1 \times 16 = 16$.
Subtract. $21 - 16 = 5$.

$$\begin{array}{r} 1 \\ 16\overline{)2154} \\ -\,16 \\ \hline 55 \end{array}$$

Bring down the 5 to make 55. You can make 3 groups of 16 ($3 \times 16 = 48$) from 55, but not 4 ($4 \times 16 = 64$).

```
     13
16)2154
  − 16
    55
  − 48
     7
```

Write a 3 above the 5.

Multiply. $3 \times 16 = 48$.

Write 48 below the 55.

Subtract. $55 - 48 = 7$.

```
     13
16)2154
  − 16
    55
  − 48
    74
```

Bring down the 4 to make 74.

You can make 4 groups of

16 ($4 \times 16 = 64$) from 74, but not

5 ($5 \times 16 = 80$).

```
    134 R10
16)2154
  − 16
    55
  − 48
    74
  − 64
    10
```

Write a 4 above the 4.

Multiply. $4 \times 16 = 64$.

Write 64 below the 74.

Subtract. $74 - 64 = 10$.

There are no more numbers to bring

down. Write a remainder of 10.

$$2154 \div 16 = 134 \text{ R}10$$

Powers of Ten

Powers of ten are any numbers that are a one followed by zeros. For example, 10, 100, and 1,000 are all powers of ten.

To divide by a power of ten, move the decimal point one place to the left for each zero at the end of the number.

$$50 \div 10 = \underline{\hspace{2cm}}$$

In whole numbers, the decimal point is at the end. Write the dividend with a decimal point at the end.

50.
decimal point

You are dividing by 10, which has one zero. So, move the decimal point one place to the left.

50.

5.0

$$50 \div 10 = 5$$

$$35,000 \div 100 = \underline{\hspace{1.5cm}}$$

Write a decimal point after the dividend.

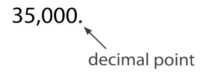

35,000.

decimal point

You are dividing by one hundred, which has two zeros. So, move the decimal point two places to the left.

35,000.

350.00

$$35,000 \div 100 = 350$$

Multiples of Ten

When both the dividend and the divisor end in zeros, you can take the same number of zeros off each and then divide.

$$250 \div 50$$

Both numbers end in one zero.
Take one zero off each number.

$$250 \div 50$$
$$25\cancel{0} \div 5\cancel{0}$$
$$25 \ \div 5$$

Now divide. The result is the same as the answer to the orginal problem.

$$25 \div 5 = 5$$

$$250 \div 50 = 5$$

Let's look at another one.

$$3,200 \div 800$$

Both numbers end in two zeros.

Take two zeros off each number.

$3200 \div 800$

$3200 \div 800$

$32 \quad \div 8$

Now divide. The result is the same as the answer to the orginal problem.

$32 \div 8 = 4$

$$3,200 \div 800 = 4$$

One basic fact can be used to find the answer for many division problems.

$24 \div 4 = 6$

$240 \div 40 = 6$

$2,400 \div 400 = 6$

$54 \div 6 = 9$

$540 \div 60 = 9$

$5,400 \div 600 = 9$

multiple of ten—The product of ten multiplied by a counting number. The multiples of ten are 10, 20, 30, 40, 50, . . .

Division and Estimation

You can use basic division facts to estimate the answer to a division problem.

$$62 \div 8$$

The division facts for 8 that have dividends close to 62 are

$$56 \div 8 = 7 \text{ and } 64 \div 8 = 8.$$

dividend ⟋   ⟍ dividend

The number 62 is closer to 64 than 56, so you can say

$$62 \div 8 \text{ is about } 8.$$

I have about 1200 eyes! Want to count them?

You can estimate the answer to a division problem with larger numbers by rounding each number to its greatest place value.

$$207 \div 19$$

If you round 207 to the hundreds place, you get 200.

The greatest place value in 19 is the tens place, so 19 rounds to 20.

$$200 \div 20$$

The numbers 200 and 20 each end in zero. You can reduce the numbers to make the problem easier.

The answer for $200 \div 20$ is the same as the answer for $20 \div 2$.

$$20 \div 2 = 10$$

$207 \div 19$ is about 10.

Properties and Division

Are the same properties true for division that are true for multiplication? Let's check.

When you multiply, you can change the order of the numbers and the answer will not change. Is this true for division?

$$9 \div 3 \qquad 3 \div 9$$

How many groups of 3 can you make from 9? 3

$$9 \div 3 = 3$$

How many groups of 9 can you make from 3? None! The number 9 is bigger than 3.

You cannot change the order of the numbers in a division problem.

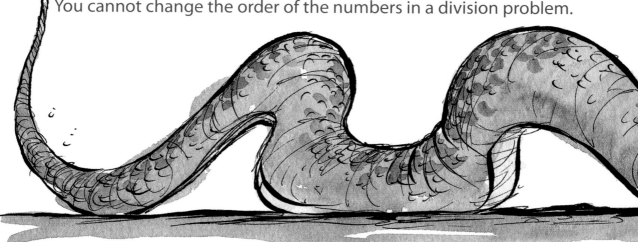

When you multiply more than two numbers, you can group the numbers in any way to multiply them. Is this true for division?

$$(60 \div 6) \div 2 \qquad 60 \div (6 \div 2)$$

Divide inside parentheses first.

$$(60 \div 6) \div 2 \qquad\qquad 60 \div (6 \div 2)$$
$$(10) \div 2 \qquad\qquad 60 \div (3)$$

Divide again.

$$10 \div 2 = 5 \qquad\qquad 60 \div 3 = 20$$
$$(60 \div 6) \div 2 = 5 \qquad\qquad 60 \div (6 \div 2) = 20$$

You cannot group the numbers any way you choose in a division problem.

I guess a rule is a rule.

Checking Your Answer

Because multiplication and division are opposite operations, you can use multiplication to check the answer to a division problem.

On page 19, we found that

$$42 \div 3 = 14$$

If $42 \div 3 = 14$ is correct, then $14 \times 3 = 42$.

$$
\begin{array}{r}
1 \\
14 \\
\times\ \ 3 \\
\hline
2
\end{array}
\qquad\qquad
\begin{array}{r}
1 \\
14 \\
\times\ \ 3 \\
\hline
42
\end{array}
$$

Multiply ones.

$3 \times 4 = 12$.

Regroup.

Multiply tens. $3 \times 1 = 3$.

Add. $3 + 1 = 4$.

$$14 \times 3 = 42, \text{ so } 42 \div 3 = 14.$$

When the answer to a division problem has a remainder, first use multiplication, then add the remainder.
On page 23, we found that

$$30 \div 9 = 3 \text{ R}3$$

divisor

Multiply the divisor and the part of the answer that is not the remainder.

$$9 \times 3 = 27$$

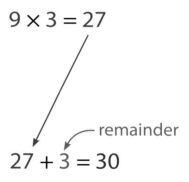

remainder

Add the remainder to the number you just found.

$$27 + 3 = 30$$

The result (30) is the same as the number you divided, so the answer is correct.

$$30 \div 9 = 3 \text{ R}3$$

Division Key Words

Owen is half as old as his sister Lauren. Lauren is 14. How old is Owen?

The word *half* tells you that you should divide by 2 to find Owen's age.

14 years ÷ 2 = 7 years
Owen is 7 years old.

Words that help you know how to solve problems are called key words. Some key words for division problems are listed in the table below.

Division Key Words		
average	equal parts	per
cut	evenly	quotient
divided	every	separate
divisor	half	shared
each	out of	split

Some division problems will ask you to change a value for more than one item to a value for one item.

If you know the:	and you need to find the:
Price of more than one	Price of one
Size of more than one	Size of one
Length of more than one	Length of one

A package of three computer games sells for $51. What is the cost per game?

Since you know the cost of three (more than one) games, you can find the cost of one game by dividing.

First write the problem in words.

cost of three games divided by three is the cost per game

$$\$51 \div 3 = \$17$$

The cost is $17 per game.

Word Problems

Word problems can be solved by following four steps.

Your club bought 168 flowers to give to 12 teachers.
Each teacher will get the same number of flowers.
How many flowers will each teacher get?

1 **Understand** the problem.

Find what you know.   There are 168 flowers and
                                       12 teachers.

Find what you want   The number of flowers
to know.   each teacher will get.

2 **Plan** how to solve the problem.

You are looking for the equal number of flowers each teacher will
get. You know the total number of flowers and the number of
teachers. This is a division problem.

3 **Solve** the problem.

Divide the number of flowers by the number of teachers.

168 flowers ÷ 12 teachers = 14 flowers per teacher.

4 **Check** your work.

Check division by multiplying.
14 flowers per teacher × 12 teachers = 168 flowers.

Understanding the Remainder

When a quotient has a remainder, you must decide what the remainder means.

Let's look at some problems that use the same facts, but ask different questions.

A coin collection book displays four coins on each page. You have collected 51 coins. How many pages will you use if you put all of the coins in the book?

You are being asked to divide your 51 coins into groups of 4.

$$51 \div 4 = 12 \text{ R}3$$

The question asks how many pages will you use. Twelve pages will be full; another page will be needed for the remaining 3 coins.

Since $12 + 1 = 13$, you will use 13 pages.

A coin collection book displays four coins on each page. You have collected 51 coins. How many pages can you fill completely?

In this problem, only the full pages are counted. You will have 12 full pages.

A coin collection book displays four coins on each page. You have collected 51 coins. How many coins will be on the last page?

In this problem, the question asks how many coins will be on the last page, which is the remainder. There will be 3 coins on the last page.

Word Problems and Remainders

Let's use the steps from pages 40 and 41 to solve a word problem that uses a remainder.

There are 2,153 chocolate candies in a bag. You get to eat what is left after the candies are divided equally into 20 bags. How many candies are you allowed to eat?

1   **Understand** the problem.

Find what you know.   There are 2,153 candies to go equally into 20 bags.

Find what you want to know.   The number of candies left over.

2   **Plan** how to solve the problem.

A large group of candies is being divided equally into smaller groups. This is a division problem.

3   **Solve** the problem.

Divide the number of candies by the number of bags.

$$2{,}153 \div 20 = 107 \text{ R}13$$

The question asks how many candies you get to eat. Since you get what is left over, or what remains, the remainder is the answer. You get to eat 13 candies.

4   **Check** your work.

When division problems have a remainder, first multiply ($107 \times 20 = 2{,}140$), then add the remainder ($2{,}140 + 13 = 2{,}153$). You are back to the original number you divided, so your answer is correct.

Further Reading

Basher, Simon, and Dan Green. *Math: A Book You Can Count On*. New York: Kingfisher, 2010.

Cleary, Brian P. *A Fraction's Goal—Part of a Whole*. Minneapolis, Minn.: Millbrook Press, 2012.

Franco, Betsy. *Funny Fairy Tale Math*. New York: Scholastic, Inc. 2011.

Mahaney, Ian. F. *Math at the Bank: Place Value and Properties of Operations*. New York: PowerKids Press, 2013.

Internet Addresses

Aplusmath. "Division Flashcards." © 1998–2012.

    <http://www.aplusmath.com/flashcards/division.html>

Minori, Carla. "Division Facts." © 1998–2012.

    <http://www.quia.com/jg/65651.html>

The Math Forum. "Ask Dr. Math." © 1994–2012.

    <http://mathforum.org/library/drmath/sets/

    elem_division.html>

Index